HOMELESS TO

UNSTOPPABLE

Journey of Resilience and Perseverance

MIKE KWON

Not everybody can be famous, but everybody can be great because greatness is determined by service.

- Martin Luther King Jr.

TABLE OF CONTENTS

DEDICATION

T his book is dedicated to everyone actively seeking to improve the lives of others and use their success to bridge the gap in this world. Regardless of our differences, we all have something valuable to offer one another. We come from diverse backgrounds and have the potential to make significant contributions to each other's lives.

The average person will live approximately 25,000 days; however, their legacy is determined by how they choose to spend each day, striving not only to live their best life but also to uplift the lives of others. Sadly, many people are overlooked today, and while Artificial Intelligence has its place, it can never replace the compassion and empathy needed to serve others. In a society where self-promotion is prevalent, showing care and inspiring others comes at no cost. We all encounter challenges, irrespective of socioeconomic status, race, sex, or ethnicity. Humans all possess emotions, feelings, and a heart; thus, we all require inspiration. Every individual, regardless of their profession or role in society, has the power to make a meaningful impact on others' lives – educators, social workers, first responders, medical professionals, military service members, coaches, mental health counselors, and parents or guardians all can affect positive change. We must commit to serving others and bringing out the best in ourselves.

ACKNOWLEDGMENTS

I am incredibly grateful to everyone who contributed to the creation and success of this book. Your unwavering support, encouragement, and expertise made this project possible. I want to express my gratitude to each of you for your love, understanding, and patience throughout this incredible journey.

Your encouragement kept me going, even during the most challenging times. I sincerely appreciate my mentors, whose guidance and wisdom have been invaluable. Your insights and advice have genuinely shaped my perspective and enriched this book. A special thank you to everybody who generously shared their stories, experiences, and expertise, enhancing this book with your valuable insights and perspectives. From the dedicated teachers and counselors to the kind-hearted individuals who guided me during a time of homelessness and the remarkable leaders and mentors who invested in me at a young age, I am deeply grateful for your influence.

I also want to express my deepest gratitude to Captain Brett Crozier for providing the foreword. Your leadership during the COVID outbreak and your impact on the lives of those 5,000

Sailors are truly commendable. I am honored to have your endorsement of my book.

Lastly, I want to thank the readers who will embark on this journey with me. Your interest and support mean the world to me, and I hope this book inspires, educates, and empowers you in your endeavors. Thank you all for being a part of this remarkable journey.

With heartfelt appreciation,

Mike Kwon

FOREWORD

With great pleasure and admiration, I introduce you to "Homeless to Unstoppable," the remarkable life story of Mike Kwon. As a former Navy Captain, I've witnessed numerous tales of resilience, determination, and leadership. Still, Mike's journey is an extraordinary testament to the human spirit's capacity to overcome adversity and soar to incredible heights.

I am blessed to have sailed and worked alongside Mike on a US aircraft carrier and witnessed him in action. He is the real deal, and I know you will enjoy your journey through these inspiring pages.

In these pages, Mike shares his deeply personal narrative, from the heart-wrenching struggles of homelessness and abandonment at a young age to his meteoric rise as a distinguished military officer and an influential life coach. His story resonates with a universal truth: that our circumstances do not define us; instead, it is our unwavering resolve, relentless perseverance, and boundless compassion that shape our destinies.

What strikes me most about Mike's journey is not just his triumphs but the profound impact he has had on the lives of others.

Throughout his experiences, he emphasizes the importance of giving back, of being the catalyst that propels someone else to greater heights. He reminds us that authentic leadership is not merely about authority or command but about genuine care, empathy, and the willingness to serve others selflessly.

Drawing from his military background, Mike beautifully illustrates the concept of being the "steam catapult" in someone's life—providing that extra push, that essential support, to help them take flight and achieve their aspirations. He pays homage to the countless individuals who served as his own steam, guiding him through life's challenges and instilling in him the values of hard work, integrity, and resilience.

As readers embark on this transformative journey with Mike, they will undoubtedly be inspired by his unwavering faith, unyielding determination, and relentless pursuit of excellence. They will learn that no obstacle is insurmountable, no dream too lofty, and that anything is possible with the right mindset and unwavering determination.

I commend Mike Kwon for his courage in sharing his story and dedication to empowering others to reach their full potential. "Homeless to Unstoppable" is more than just a memoir; it is a beacon of hope, a testament to the indomitable human spirit, and a powerful reminder that within each of us lies the power to overcome, inspire, and be truly unstoppable.

Captain Brett Crozier, US Navy Retired

Former helicopter pilot, fighter pilot, commanding officer of a US aircraft carrier, and author of Surf When You Can: Lessons in Life, Leadership, and Loyalty from a Maverick Navy Captain

INTRODUCTION

When people first meet me, they see the "end" product – they have no idea about the process it took for me to arrive at this place. I certainly "don't look like" I've been through the life I've been to this point. In this book, I want to share some foundational elements of my life that helped define and shape the man I am today. I want my story to inspire you and empower you to believe that just because you hit rock bottom doesn't mean you have to give up – the significant part of hitting rock bottom is that there is no place else to go but up. My life story is a tale of perseverance, resilience, tenacity, and hope – all critical elements of effective leadership. Enjoy, learn, and embrace my words – you're in for a good story.

I am resilient and capable of overcoming any challenge that comes my way.

CHAPTER 1

MY NEW ADDRESS

Sometimes, when people hear that someone was raised in the "projects," their immediate reaction is contempt. For some reason, there's always a negative connotation associated with life in concrete neighborhood communities. In many instances, this negative connotation is far from the truth, as these communities help to motivate and propel residents toward a better life. In addition, these communities provide sufficient shelter so residents would not have to resort to the alternative of living on the streets.

For me, "project life" was where I felt like I was part of a diverse community of good people who may have been economically impoverished but did not suffer from emotional and intellectual poverty. The bond was not defined by race, class, or gender. Instead, it thrived on community values and beliefs. For me, it was a place that I called home for many years.

Playing handball, freeze-tag, football, and baseball on the streets of New York City was a daily pastime that filled our hearts. We made the word "fun" work for us. On any day, the sidewalks and courtyards were full of children smiling, laughing, running, jumping, and playing while believing in what we could not see and playing with the courage and tenacity needed to win. At the same time, parents stood nearby chatting with friends about their daily lives, hopes, dreams deferred, and perhaps, their struggles for significance. Community. That's what it was, and life, for me, felt good until it wasn't anymore.

My mom worked hard for the two of us — sometimes holding down three jobs at a time, being paid "under the table" to earn enough money to pay the rent. Many days, my only meals came from school: breakfast and lunch. And then I would return home without so much hot water to a table, knowing full well that I wouldn't be eating dinner. As a 13-year-old eighth grader, I didn't have school supplies and would show up to school with shoes that had holes in the soles. Although embarrassed, I never complained because I was with someone who loved me and a community where I was accepted. But it all came to a screeching halt when my mother could no longer work because of her severe back pain. Beyond the physical impact, her disability paralyzed our entire lives because she was unable to work. Eventually, we were evicted from our apartment in the projects. The eviction helped me to realize that although we lived in substandard housing and poverty, we had everything because we had each other, whereas living in the outside world made us feel as though we had nothing.

Initially, my mom didn't give up because she believed someone would help us. And, in the beginning, she was right. We received some short-term assistance, but it didn't stretch far enough because we had to move into a shelter. Still, as a woman of faith and believer in God, my mom was devoted to her church and "the miracles God bestowed upon man." We went to church every Sunday, and she spent countless hours volunteering her time and talents. She always said, "Even though you have nothing, there's always room to serve." Through daily lessons, she taught me the power of sharing with others. If I had only one piece of candy, my mother would encourage me to share it with my friends because she believed even if you were poor, you were responsible for sharing your poverty. The power of serving man was necessary when you were serving God. She served through the church and raised me to believe there's always a way to serve.

But, when we began to hit rock bottom, I wondered, at what point would the church serve us? When will we "reap what we sow?" When we needed a place to live, they didn't help. When we needed to eat, it was limited. "The Church" failed my mother and me, and soon, the life we knew was over. The community we were a part of had disappeared, so the subway stations became our new address.

My mom felt defeated as we rode trains during the day and slept on the subway platforms at night. Since she could no longer work and provide for us, we would go weeks without a decent meal. We survived on only scraps of food left by others in the trash cans. She began trying to convince me that I was better off without her and that she had failed me as a mother, but I never believed that. I told her I would rather be hungry and poor than live without her. She said she loved me enough to let me go live with someone else so they could provide for me. I pleaded with her to stick it out and keep fighting; we would figure it out because I only wanted to be with her.

I thought my words had brought at least a little comfort to her and that my presence was enough for her to believe that everything would be okay – it wasn't. One morning, when I awakened at the train station, my mom was nowhere to be found. At first, I thought she left to find us food or money. Then, as the minutes turned into hours and the hours morphed into days, I realized my mother was never returning. Abandoned, scared, confused, bewildered, and alone, I had to decide to take care of myself the best way I knew how. It was just "me, myself, and I," and "we" had to figure out life together if I was going to survive on the streets of New York City. The Metropolitan Transit Authority became the place I called "home." It gave me warmth, shelter, and food from the trash on the good days.

As a thirteen-year-old boy, I was faced with too many disappointments simultaneously. I felt powerless and worthless because I couldn't help my mom; now, the 9/11 terrorist attacks destroyed my city, and I could do nothing about it. The experience was too much for me to endure, so I questioned the reality I was suddenly thrust into, but at the same time, I also wanted to fight for my future. I couldn't fight for my mom because she chose to leave, but the urge to fight for my country began to blossom at that point. I felt stronger because the attacks showed me what happens when a country is unprepared – terrorists attack you and everything important to you. I was unprepared when my mother left me while I slept, and the United States was unprepared when the attacks occurred. I vowed always to work my hardest to be prepared for whatever I may face.

By chance, I was fortunate to meet a man who owned a warehouse, and he allowed me and other homeless teens to sleep in the warehouse at night. There was no heat or hot water, but we had a roof over our heads and slept on cardboard boxes. Every day, I roamed the streets of New York with a purpose – to make money and find food because I deserved it. But it took a chance meeting with a despicable man to help me learn this lesson. As I watched him eat a slice of pizza from a short distance away and noticed he was about to throw away some scraps, I approached him and asked if I could have them. He rudely snarled, "No!" He put the rest in a brown paper bag, crumpled it, and threw it into a nearby trash can. He looked at me like I belonged in that trash can; me, a homeless and hungry 13-year-old kid. My spirit was shattered, and my soul was defeated as I returned to the warehouse that night.

Sitting cross-legged on my makeshift bed and watching all the other hungry kids, I began questioning my identity. Am I real? Am I invisible? Am I human? Am I worthless? What about me made that man seemingly take pleasure in throwing away his scraps in my face when he could see a hungry child standing in front of him? All these questions danced in my mind when, finally, a light bulb flickered on. As terrible a human as that man was, he gave me an invaluable experience that brought me to a profound realization – I must take control of my future and create my opportunities. I must prepare for whatever each day brings because I'm responsible for caring for myself.

At first, I tried to follow my mother's rules, but they didn't seem to work anymore. So, I quickly learned that the struggle for significance and survival was not always done in the "right" way. Instead, I had to be strategic, intentional, and incredibly diligent. There was no time to focus on losing family, identity, self-worth, and confidence because the challenge of finding my next meal became the focus every day. I was in crisis mode and struggling for survival, so I became creative and stole food. If I had to choose the lesser of the two evils – stealing felt better than begging at the time because I could do it without feeling that same shame I felt when that selfish man threw the pizza away in my face.

I had to take control of my circumstances and create chances to thrive because it would never happen if I waited for the world around me to do it. I didn't need the universe's permission to be successful in the survival game. I equipped and empowered myself with the creativity needed to win at living – and it worked.

FOOD FOR THOUGHT

Reflect on a time when you faced a significant challenge. How did you overcome it, and what did you learn from the experience?

_____

_____

_____

_____

_____

_____

_____

_____

_____

_____

_____

_____

_____

_____

_____

_____

_____

_____

_____

_____

_____

_____

_____

I am worthy of love, success, and happiness.

CHAPTER 2

A GAME OF CARDS

When people ask me about the details of my life, I often stop and pause. I hesitate because there are so many complicated layers to my life that I cannot explain, let alone someone truly comprehend. Honestly, most of the time, I don't want to describe or relive it. So, I've learned over the years to equate it to a game of cards—you never know the hand you are dealt, but if you want to win, you need to learn how to play the game, understand all the rules and the best way to take advantage of whatever circumstances your opponents present.

That's it.

My warehouse comrades quickly became my family because we looked out for one another – it became an "all for one, and one for all" pact. We shared a physical and somewhat emotional space because the outside world could not comprehend what we were going through. The experience was unique and inexplicable to others because no one could or would believe that so many abandoned teenagers lived on the streets of New York City. Many would've assumed we had family members who could care for us even if our parents could not. The truth was, we didn't. Our only family was the one we created in the warehouse, and we had to look out and fight for the well-being of one another.

Inside the warehouse, there was a kid named Aaron. The interesting thing about Aaron was that he was a bright young kid. One day, I asked him, "Hey, when is your birthday?" And he said, "I don't know my birthday. I lost my parents when I was really small. This warehouse is all I know, and the people here." I replied, "Man, that's horrible. You never even got a birthday gift, or nobody even sang you a birthday song or anything like that?" He shook his head no. I don't know; that was one of the first times I felt heartbroken for someone else. And I still don't quite understand what made a 13-year-old want to do this. But I hustled out there that day and was able to scrap enough together to get him a 99-cent yo-yo. And I presented it to him and said, "Hey, man, I don't know when your birthday is, but it's today, and I wanted to give you this gift." I said happy birthday to him. I remember him just crying and hugging me and just thanking me. To him, I was a hero that day. And, despite all the accomplishments I would later go on to in life and career, leadership awards, degrees, and real estate investment, I still believe that was one of my best moments. Because to make an impact on somebody at that age meant the world to me. Seeing someone smile, tear up, and be excited meant the world. A simple yo-yo and act of service made a difference.

Leading at a young age and leading the pack were roles I never anticipated, but I inherited them nonetheless. I met dozens of kids between 8 and 13 years old. Without formal leadership knowledge, I assumed the big brother role—to protect, feed, and find avenues for success. Success for us meant finding a leftover meal; it meant hustling for the basics that others took for granted every day.

As I remember living on the gritty streets, I remember getting the boys together and watching their hungry faces as we created a plan to find food. This was a new area for us, and we were uncertain how to do it. I could see that they were afraid. But I also knew someone had to take the first step, so I stepped up to lead the charge because I knew fear would cripple us. I told them I would find the food for all of us alone. I accepted the leadership position, and at that tender young age, I learned that sometimes leaders must make critical decisions and, if necessary, act alone to execute plans.

The days were grueling, and as I maneuvered my way through the streets, engaging in several illegal activities to find food for my tribe, there were times when I wanted to give up. But then I remembered the looks on their hungry faces, which motivated me to achieve the goal. Returning to the warehouse and seeing their excitement and gratitude made every risk worthwhile. It was a small victory in a world full of struggle and strife.

Soon, several other boys found the courage to follow me into the streets to search for our food. I asked them why they were willing to risk everything to follow me; their answer was simple, "Because we've got your back and you sacrificed for us." From that moment on, our familial connection was stronger than blood because it was a brotherhood created from adversity. It was a "ride or die" relationship -- a commitment we made to stand by each other through thick and thin. Navigating alleys, understanding routes, and assessing opponents became daily challenges. Failure was frequent, but it wasn't an option. We had to outsmart our opponents and maximize our resources to survive another day—to give ourselves a chance to win. And we did it together as brothers.

Looking back, I realize that those early years on the streets taught me invaluable leadership lessons I couldn't fully comprehend then. Street tactics became second nature, and I learned to navigate the complexities of human relationships with finesse and intuition. But most importantly, I discovered the true meaning of leadership: the ability to inspire loyalty, instill trust, and lead by example, even in the face of impossible odds.

Some people go through life without ever truly experiencing the depths of adversity, never tasting the bitter sting of defeat. But for me, the hurt locker was a constant companion, a place of growth and transformation. In those moments of struggle and strife, I discovered the true meaning of grit. It taught me that true strength isn't measured by the absence of pain but by the ability to endure, overcome, and emerge stronger on the other side. I had learned to be a good card player, and my survival strategies worked – until they didn't anymore.

One day, while on the streets, a neighborhood police officer questioned me about my daily activities. He noted that he and fellow officers had watched me for a while and noticed that I was never in school during the day. He told me that because of my age, attendance in school was mandatory. If I were genuinely homeless, he would need to remove me from the warehouse and place me in a facility with other homeless teens. And he did.

The day I left the warehouse and entered the youth center, a new life began for me. I couldn't remember the last time I slept in a real bed; I had a twin bed in the facility. Not only did I have my bed, but I ate three meals every day, freeing me from the hustling and grinding I was used to going through every single day. I didn't have to worry about where the next meal came from; it felt good.

I was surrounded by other diligent, energetic, and brilliant souls who shared the common goal of wanting to be a part of a family. We built a camaraderie because we all shared and understood the feelings of abandonment, isolation, fear, confusion, and doubt. We also knew, however, that the ultimate dream was to be accepted by a family. So, while we built a team, we also rooted for anyone who found a "forever" home. That would take time, and I would have to learn how to deal with many emotions.

My life has been a game of cards since I first learned how to play when I was about fourteen or fifteen years old, living in a juvenile detention center for abandoned youth in lower Manhattan in the 1990s with other homeless teenagers. Just like the old warehouse where I used to live, we were rejected and left to stand alone without the care of those who brought us into this world. But unlike our prior place of refuge, we were not inanimate objects placed amongst "things." Instead, we were alive, living, and breathing, with thoughts, feelings, and emotions. But while there, the other teens taught me how to play the card game "Spades." Learning how to play this game and winning was pivotal to my mindset. A game of cards changed my life.

A Social Worker (I'll call her Agent Ross) was assigned to my case and visited me several times, but only shared terrible news each time – nobody wanted me. I told myself not being chosen was okay and tried to act as though being accepted wasn't necessary. However, I secretly felt lost and abandoned again with every "No" I received, so I began questioning my identity, who I was, and why this was happening. It didn't make sense to be a teenager with no one to love me. I started to question if I was worthy of love. I felt helpless and hopeless, and the struggle for significance felt overwhelming, but I didn't know what to do.

After some time had passed, Agent Ross told me there was an elderly couple who wanted to open their home to me, so I left the center to live with Bob and his family. This experience was a critical shift in my life because Bob fostered several other teens and me and gave us a place to call "home." They treated us with dignity and respect and encouraged us to be the best version of ourselves as we fought for our dreams.

Agent Ross approached me and said, "Hey, are you ready to pack your stuff? Your foster care parents are here to pick you up." I told her I had nothing to pack as I wore only clothes I owned. I was ready to go. A lot went through my mind as we walked outside the brick building. Who is this person? What do they look like? Everyone has rejected me. Who is this hero about to pick me up from the streets?

I saw a minivan pull up, and as the door opened, I saw a Black American man walking toward me. I hesitated for a moment, not because I was racist, but because I was confused and uncertain if this was the person who chose me, someone who didn't look like me at all. And if so, what made him choose me? We got into the car, and he was super friendly to me. He asked if we needed extra clothes and mentioned going shopping at Kmart. I told him I had no money, and he said, "I can't believe that's a 13-year-old's answer! No worries about money; I'll help you."

Living in Mr. Bob's house was vastly different from my previous life. Living first-hand with Black culture, language, accent, and food – was all different from what I **was** used to. But they were kind, believers in God, and amazing people willing to help me. There were seven to ten other kids, and I was the only Asian kid in the house. Despite feeling like I didn't fit in at times, this new experience taught me tremendously throughout my life and made me a better leader.

Looking back, I realize I led and connected with many people because of this experience. Most people may not understand the value of respecting different cultures or understanding and appreciating one another's culture. But for me, I got to live it. Even though I didn't choose it alone, I had that opportunity through God's grace. I deeply appreciate the Black community and what they endure daily. I profoundly respect that since I could see it first-hand with what Bob and the other kids dealt with daily.

I remember one day, Bob asked me to come down to his living room, and we ended up having a fireside chat. Curfew typically meant that everyone had to be in their beds by 10 o'clock, but he broke the rule just for me that day. He explained that he wanted to have a special talk with me, and we ended up having a really good conversation. He started by asking how I was doing and how I was feeling. This was one of the first times that someone had ever asked me how I was doing as a person, as a human being. After having spent so much time living on the streets, Bob's concern for and interest in me felt very authentic but surreal at the same time. He asked me what I was thinking. I said, "Hey Bob, what made you accept me? I was rejected three times: the City of New York, my mother, and everyone abandoned me. Everyone walked away; no one helped me. Why did you accept me? I felt like I didn't fit in here. I'm the only Asian kid here. I don't look like any of them here. I don't look like you. Why did you accept me?" I was hoping for a million-dollar answer. Bob said, "Well, first off, don't ever say that. Don't ever say you don't fit in. Don't ever say no one cares for you. I didn't care about your skin color, your race, or how much money was in your pocket. All I cared about was that there was a kid in need, and I wanted to take you off the street to give you a fighting chance to have a life." To me, that meant the world. Those words were inspirational; they lit a fire within my soul that helped me going for all these years.

That conversation helped me understand that words matter more than most people can fathom. They have the potential to make a change in someone's life, in their perspective, and in one's outcome of success in life. Later that night, Bob showed me his left hand, and two rings were on it. He mentioned one was his wedding ring, and the other was passed down from his father. He explained his concerns about not having kids and always wondered whom he would pass it to. Shortly after, he pulled out the ring and gave it to me. I was shocked and lost for words that someone like me would receive such a ring with significance.

He told me he believed in me and that I had a bright future. He mentioned that where I start in life doesn't mean that's where I have to finish in life. That day, I cried. Keep in mind I never cried when my mom left me; I never cried when I got beat up; I never cried when people told me that I got rejected, and I never cried when the City of New York abandoned me. But for some reason, that day, I cried.

Bob gave me hope again because he believed in me and my dreams. I finally began to trust the world again and soon felt like I belonged while living with Bob. He was the family I dreamed about and craved for while living on the streets of New York. But, of course, this living arrangement would change, too, because in foster care, inevitably, it's not a "forever" placement, and changes happen. Once my paternal family was found, Bob told me I would have to move to California to live with them.

Here we go again. My voice was silenced, my opinion was marginalized, and my bags were packed without my approval. I was tired of all this change, this constant uprooting of my life. So, I decided that others would no longer have that power and control over me and my life. I would learn a new game of cards to control the hand I had been dealt. I was forced to leave the supportive family I had grown to love and was off to a different world with a different mindset. I would be ready.

I was prepared but still angry about these new circumstances when I arrived in California. I was furious at the world because, again, the world abandoned me. The government took me from my family with Bob and placed me with a new family in California. Although very kind and generous, those "real" family members were strangers to me. I never trusted people I did not know. But did the government care? Nope. They separated me from the only safe and secure environment I had had for years – and I was mad about it.

The new family enrolled me in the local high school, but because I was so far behind, the school counselor tried to convince me to drop out and work towards earning a GED. As I listened, I felt my heart sink into my lap because, once again, someone told me I wasn't good enough. Someone didn't think I was worthy to achieve success and only saw me as a piece of trash, some burden they'd rather not spend the time or effort trying to help. Maybe she was trying to be realistic with me, but the experience felt like rejection all over again, and it hurt because no one understood my story and what I had gone through in my life. I didn't ask for the circumstances that pushed me behind in school, but I was still penalized. I was the "dumb guy" by default. I wasn't dumb– they didn't know who I was or my history.

Feeling defeated and trying to decide my next steps, another counselor approached me and said she had overheard the previous conversation. However, she gave me hope because she described another way to earn my high school diploma. Although it was a long shot, she explained the process and told me exactly what to do. She was a hero to me in some ways because although she didn't know me, she understood my dream and took extra steps to help me achieve the dream.

The recommendation was to enroll in an adult learning course, but I would need a job to earn money to pay for it because it wasn't free. I found a job working in a local store late at night as a stock boy, and the great thing about the job was the owner paid me in advance so I could pay the tuition for the school. I attended classes during the day and worked at night for a year and a half – I completed 2½ years of high school in a year and a half. I was determined to receive a high school diploma because I wanted to enlist in the military and needed it to reach that goal.

The Armed Services Office was across the street from my high school, so that I would pass it daily. One day, a Marine Sergeant approached me and shared the promotional information, and I told him I was interested. I told him I was ready to sign up immediately, so he took me to the Armed Services Vocational Aptitude Battery (ASVAB) military entrance exam. After completing it, he noted that I could return later to discuss the results.

When I returned, the Marine Sergeant was unavailable, but a Naval Chief stood in front of the building and asked why I had come to the office. I told him I found out that I had passed the ASVAB and was ready to serve my country. Confused, he asked why I was so eager to join the military. I told him, "I just want an opportunity to do something." Of course, he wanted to know more, so I shared that September 11, 2001, was perhaps the worst catastrophe in the United States that had an impact on the entire world. The terror attack on this country attempted to dismantle the pride, joy, and honor of being an American citizen, and I was furious and wanted to do something about it. After sharing that I lived in New York City during and after the 9/11 attack, I felt obligated to protect and serve my country.

The Chief began sharing details about the Navy and asked if I was interested. I told him the military branch didn't matter and he could ship me anywhere because I didn't care. Shocked, he said, "Wow, you are the easiest and most motivated guy I've ever had to sign up!" I laughed and told him I just wanted to chase the bad guys; I needed the opportunity to do it, and I craved to do something with my life. I signed all the paperwork he needed that day and only needed my diploma. When I finally completed the high school graduation requirements, an office assistant printed an official transcript and gave it to the recruiter, and that's how my military career began.

FOOD FOR THOUGHT

Write about a time when someone said something that made a massive difference in your life and why it mattered.

_____

_____

_____

_____

_____

_____

_____

_____

_____

_____

_____

_____

_____

_____

_____

_____

_____

_____

_____

_____

_____

_____

_____

_____

I trust in life, knowing that everything happens for a reason.

CHAPTER 3

WHEN YOU CLIMB THE LADDER, SMELL THE ROSES

When I arrived at boot camp, I was self-confident and mentally prepared. After my life experiences, I knew I could handle anything. Bootcamp gave me an adrenaline rush that influenced me to want to do more. My drill instructors couldn't understand why I constantly smiled — they didn't understand how the military had just saved my life. I didn't want or need anything else because working provided everything I believed equipped and empowered me to be the best man possible. I had clothes on my back, food in my belly, a bed to lay my head on at night, and a mission that drove me to protect the country. What else could I ask for?

Jason Blankenship was my first leader in the United States Navy. He had served almost 20 years and was ready to retire when I met him during my first deployment aboard USS ABRAHAM LINCOLN (CVN 72). He would come into Arresting Gear Engine

#3 each night and read a thick manual. Also known as the target wire or "three-wire," is the ideal spot for pilots to target when landing onboard a nuclear-powered aircraft carrier. As such, it was where the ship typically placed the most trusted operator, which I was fortunate enough to have become by that time. I asked Chief Blankenship about the length of time he had served in the military. He gave me a rundown of his entire career. Shocked, I said, "Wow! You must know everything about this equipment and still read the same manual?" He responded, "No matter how many times I've read this thing and how many times I have done this maintenance, I always read and brush up on the material to learn something new so that I never become complacent." He continued by sharing, "If I expect my people to read and perform at a high level, then I should read along with them. That makes someone a 'subject matter expert' and, in my eyes, a phenomenal leader."

To this day, I navigate challenges by reading, learning, and always being a step ahead of everyone. Life is about preparation, and often, we have too many people taking shortcuts and too many people expecting others to hold a standard. Unfortunately, most people seem to want things handed to them. Now, they rely on artificial intelligence to solve life's problems. Reality is instrumental in solving life's problems, so experience can never be substituted. Experience allows you to explain the processes by offering value and information to individuals or organizations. While stationed, I worked hard, and the results of my labor started to get noticed by my supervisors. I qualified for several higher pay grades/ranks and achieved them quickly, but I was not allowed to become a supervisor because I was too young. The military system put a cap on my achievements based on my age and time. It was frustrating because I passed all the qualifying exams but was still limited in my promotions. But you know what? I kept working hard because I believed doing so would make a difference once I held the momentum. And it did.

Chief Warrant Officer 2 (CWO2) John Federico was my first Aircraft Launch and Recovery Equipment (ALRE) Maintenance Officer on the LINCOLN. He was responsible for 255 men and women to safely launch and recover aircraft aboard a carrier in the middle of the ocean. He had over 20 years of experience. When I first entered the Navy as a junior sailor at the rank of E-1 (Airman Recruit), the norm was never to speak to an E-5 (2nd Class Petty Officer) or above. Junior leadership completed most of the work. If you were in trouble, a superior told you to stand at attention and pop tall before them. However, one day, I had an opportunity to meet John for a qualification board. I had to stand before him and other highly qualified leaders, including three Senior Chiefs with over two decades of service. They drilled me for 3½ hours with question after question. After the final board meeting, my maintenance officer spoke to me for the first time and said, "Airman Kwon, I am incredibly proud of you for not missing a single question asked in this room. Most would fail or miss many questions. So for you to do your diligence and master your craft, I am super proud of you." From then on, he would always follow up, mentor, and guide me to work towards the next milestone, eventually leading to my qualification as a systems expert. I was only 18 and earned my qualifications in approximately four months. Typically, it takes people four to eight years to achieve these milestones, but because of my work ethic, commitment to excellence, determination, and thoroughness, I met the standard to become a Catapult and Arresting Gear expert to handle multi-million-dollar equipment.

One day, John pulled me aside and said, "I would like you to get your Safe for flight qualification." Naturally, I informed him the instruction wouldn't allow me to do so because it's a senior pay grade qualification. He told me he would submit a waiver for me to the carrier's Commanding Officer and submit it off the ship to Air Pacific Fleet Command for final approval. This blew my mind, and I asked myself how someone could have that much confidence in me and why he would take such a risk with a kid who grew up with nothing. I was just a regular young guy doing my best. Was I the best? Did my work demonstrate what being the best looked like?

We soon discovered that John's waiver submission was a wildly unpopular decision and was the first time in the history of Naval Aviation Enterprise anyone had requested the waiver. But it was approved because I had illustrated my competence to such a high degree. I became a Safe for Flight authority to certify an entire ALRE System as safe to operate. The nation's most significant weapons systems were now in the hands of a new young leader — me! Two weeks later, John sent a designation letter that announced my promotion to the work center. I was the youngest to become the supervisor for five major work centers as an E-1. This was the start of my journey as a supervisor in a leadership position on my first deployment at 18 years old — a position historically reserved for seniors with at least eight years of experience.

I remember the day I walked over to him and thanked him for the opportunity. He responded, "My job as a leader is to train, mentor, and see something good in you. It's my responsibility to ensure you are equipped with the correct tools." He then pointed to his chair and said, "Someday you will be leading the way, and it's not a matter of 'if' but 'when' you sit there. I hope you are the one to take care of people the right way." At that moment, my heart was sold to the United States Navy, and I knew our country would have my unwavering commitment. The machines, manuals, and equipment don't make the Navy great; the people who inspire and bring out the best in others are what makes the Navy great. I didn't know what he saw in me, but whatever it was, it made him train me for war. He didn't allow me to skip the process, nor did he make everything complicated, but he guided me simultaneously. This is what many call "tough love."

You see, I believe you should always do the right thing. Give it your all, whether you get the promotion or not. People want to do the work and get paid, but sometimes, we don't get paid what we think we are worth. What I have learned, however, is that my willingness to do more, regardless of whether I received the credit and whose responsibility it belonged to, made me a better leader. Many people want to get to the next level but never master their craft. Not doing so will limit your possibilities, and you will never rise above the average colleague.

Years later, I asked John why he decided to promote me. He said, "I asked the leadership team if we had to pick only one person who displays leadership and is the most knowledgeable and trustworthy, regardless of rank, whom would they choose? Unanimously, they said, 'Kwon.'" He told me, "That's the day you changed the game and proved to everyone that the instruction needed to be revised, and it's not about the pay grade but who you are." Many people wanted the promotion but were unwilling to work or weren't competent enough and didn't take the time to study to improve. My personal experience is a great lesson to help you understand that regardless of where you come from or what you've been through, you should commit to growing, learning, and pursuing your dreams. If you trust the process and do your part, a leader like John will care for the rest.

When I initially received my promotion, I thought, "Wow! My dreams were finally coming true!" I was controlling my life and making a difference for my country. I didn't know I needed anything else but more promotions. Higher-ranked guys were annoyed because they didn't want a Sailor of lower rank supervising them. I was okay with that because I knew they didn't understand my process of grit, grind, and an insatiable desire to be successful in securing my future. My ambition wasn't about them – it was about me getting things done and achieving my goals. And it worked.

This was a pivotal time in my life as a young adult because, initially, no one knew my name, but now my name was known because of my achievements. I finally felt worthy and essential – as though I mattered. I saw how my contributions made a real-world difference and began to get recognized because of it. Things changed; my responsibility level increased as I supervised 55 other Sailors. The more responsibility I received, the more fascinated I became, and it inspired me to want to continue to improve. My life was work, and work had become my life. It was all that mattered to me. Success and achievement were my passion projects, and I spent every waking moment pursuing them.

My second maintenance officer, Josh Stehr, I met about a year later when I was established, and he gave me the charge of supervising 65 Sailors as the Leading Petty Officer at just 19 years old. He recognized my abilities, dedication, and commitment and decided I should lead a larger group of Sailors. Historically reserved for a higher-ranked member, I was hand-picked to lead these Sailors. It was a pivotal career game-changer for me and proved that I could achieve all my goals if I worked hard. But at what cost?

I didn't have personal relationships with others because I thought it was a waste of time when I could work on my goals. I didn't have time to socialize or maintain relationships because my mental and physical bandwidth could not stretch beyond my military commitment. My heart and ego felt good because my supervisors trusted and believed in me. I had felt invisible for so many years – as though I was not good enough to be a productive citizen of society. When I joined the Navy, I proved myself wrong because I was an excellent Sailor, and my country needed me and relied on me to complete any task assigned to me. My limiting beliefs no longer had a stronghold on me.

Years later, when I came across Josh again, I asked him why he decided to promote me. He said, "Because you are reliable." He explained that trust is reliability, and he could rely on me to get things done. Josh believed being trustworthy was a critical aspect of leadership, and he believed I illustrated that trait. The funny thing is that I didn't know where I learned it – growing up, no one was reliable for me. My mom left me so that I couldn't rely on her. I couldn't rely on strangers to help feed and clothe me, and the foster care system only provided it because they were required to. So, how did I become reliable for others? How did I climb this ladder of success so quickly? I learned I didn't have to climb the ladder alone.

I had an opportunity to serve as a military boot camp drill instructor at the age of 22 in Great Lakes, Illinois. During the intensive training to become a drill instructor, part of our job was to shadow another instructor. I had the privilege to shadow the best of the best leaders; her name is CWO2 Aneesah McDowell. At that time, she was an E-6 (1st Class Petty Officer) and had been enlisted for six years in the Navy; I was also an E-6. The thing about life is that everyone meets their match when you feel like you are in your prime and think you are the best at Physical Training (PT), making rank fast, and the sharpest person around. And for me, I met my match in her. Just how she carried herself, ran PT, sang military cadences, and worked long hours from 0400-2300 daily to train the recruits was stirring. But the most fascinating part of her leadership was the ability to inspire her recruits. Motivating a group of 88 recruits in one setting in the most challenging place takes a unique person. She set the standard, so I looked up to her as a mentor for many years.

At 26 years old, I was promoted to lead a larger division of 255 Sailors. I recognized that some of the "street" skills I learned as a "warehouse kid" allowed me to lead with a style that flourished. I loved leading people who came from all walks of life – it was an honor to see them thrive and grow to become the best versions of themselves. I believed my destiny was to lead them, so I did it with my heart and soul. I often functioned without sleeping as I prepared our equipment for the following day. People would always ask, "How do you go days without sleeping?" my response was always the same – "It's because of GRIT. You need to be relentless to push through, and as a leader, I need to be where you are – working." I believed that as their leader, I shouldn't tell them to do anything I wasn't willing to do. I think it stemmed from living in the warehouse with the other kids.

As the leader of my warehouse family, I couldn't ask them to go and steal food if I wasn't willing to do it. As the crew leader, I thought I should paint with them if they had to paint the ship. If they had to pick up trash, I needed to pick it up with them because people need to see and feel their leaders guiding them. Sometimes, that means getting in the trenches with them to do the work. To be a cohesive unit, everybody must feed off the same energy, despite their rank. As a leader, sometimes that means sacrificing your time to mentor others. As a military leader, you must sacrifice some of your free time to ensure your team is best prepared for the mission.

If you are a good leader, you'll probably never get paid enough for all you do and the duties and people you're responsible for, so you must do it because you love it. It must be in your heart because everyone signs up for success, but not inconvenience. This is important because, as a leader, you will be inconvenienced more often than successful, and you still need the heart to do the job. Learning and watching my role models taught me this. When I think of my "Battle Buddy," CWO2 Aneesah McDowell, she epitomizes an excellent leader. I was blessed to have a colleague.

She never took her foot off the pedal and was willing to help me when needed. We all need someone to run the race with, and sometimes, it's okay to have a colleague and recognize that someone is more talented than you are, but it's still okay to ask for help. I want you to know that you should let the ego go because it can be your worst enemy. You cannot climb the ladder of success as a "lone wolf." Sometimes, you need to ask for help – and just because you ask for help doesn't mean that you are weak; it just means that you need help. That's a lesson I learned and permitted myself to accept it.

In retrospect, I think my military success was easy because few emotions were involved. I didn't have to free myself from the bondage of hurtful relationships and people because my worthiness was determined by the work I produced. But did I miss something? Did I miss the fun of life because I was focused on the rapid ascension to success? Did I miss out on healthy relationships? Smiles, laughter, and relaxation while I struggled for significance and found it through military ranks. Were there any roses I failed to see while climbing the ladder of success? Probably so. But if I never saw them, how could I smell them?

FOOD FOR THOUGHT

What role does perseverance play in achieving your goals? How do you maintain motivation during challenging times?

_____

_____

_____

_____

_____

_____

_____

_____

_____

_____

_____

_____

_____

_____

_____

_____

_____

_____

_____

_____

_____

_____

I forgive myself for any mistakes
and release any lingering guilt or shame.

CHAPTER 4

A HERO AIN'T NOTHIN' BUT A SANDWICH

The book A Hero Ain't Nothin' but a Sandwich, by Alice Childress, suggests there are no simple answers to more significant problems people face when surrounded by negativity. No single individual can "save" someone – life is too complicated. For me, this made sense because I never believed I had a "hero" until I met the counselor who changed the trajectory of my life when I was 17 years old. But, by then, I had already learned that I had to save myself and depend on myself as I struggled for significance. I did this by becoming resilient.

The one lesson I learned as a teenager is what I shared in the prologue: the great thing about hitting rock bottom is that there's no place to go but up. If you're at your lowest, the best must be coming because the worst has already arrived. I slept on subway cars and in train stations. Moving into an abandoned warehouse and sleeping on cardboard boxes was a step up for me and another training ground for resiliency. I repeatedly heard the word "No!" and it taught me to use it as the starting point of change. Hearing the word so often pushed me harder and forced me to work smarter as I grew up. I had to because it was the only way to survive.

If someone told me, "No, I'm not giving it to you!" After I begged for food or money, there was no flexibility to give up. I had to move on and use the "No!" as the stimulant for me to work harder for the "Yes." My life depended on it, so I kept pushing through all the "Nos" until I eventually stumbled upon a few "Yeses." I had to figure out how to win every day because my next meal depended on it. I had to teach myself that I was worth every "Yes" I earned. I needed to understand my value and worth to meet my goals and keep fighting for them. The military was a perfect fit for me; it wasn't personal but based on proving the value you brought to your unit. Your background and previous experience do not determine your worth. Instead, the grit and grind you produced daily was the source of judgment. I learned to become my hero – the person I could look up to, count on, and depend on to meet my goals.

When my military leaders showed that they trusted me and promoted me to unit leader, I knew they believed in me. From that, I began to believe in myself and understand that being valued felt good. Knowing that an institution such as the military trusted me inspired me to continue to work smarter and prove myself because I knew there were rewards for accomplishing tasks. I was fortunate to have met several people in the Navy who taught me some of the most significant lessons in my life so I could become my hero and an effective leader. I want to share some of those lessons with you below now:

I remember winning one of the top military awards, Sailor of the Year and Aviation of the Year, because of my stellar leadership. Thousands of sailors competed for the award, but I was chosen. Wow. Lil' ol' me? The kid who had to drop out of school at twelve years old. The one who had to attend an adult learning course to graduate high school? The guy who struggled with reading and writing? For a bit, it was hard to embrace that I had won, but then I remembered that despite my "layered" past, I had become a Sailor who had earned his degree, managed 250 others to care for multimillion-dollar equipment, catapults, and arresting gear while managing a budget of millions of dollars for the United States Navy. As the youngest drill instructor at 22 years old, I was also the guy out there making a difference in the lives of others and training the recruits. All of this was recognized when I won the award. It took me a minute to accept that I deserved it because I still struggled to understand my value. There were times when I believed that I didn't deserve positive reinforcement, respect, love, etc., because I was "just a warehouse kid."

The first time I boarded a plane headed to a paid speaking engagement, I walked right by my first-class seat despite matching the number on my boarding pass with the seat number. My mindset made me believe I didn't deserve that seat, so it couldn't have belonged to me. But, as I settled into that seat and allowed myself to be present in the moment, I thought about everything it took to place me in that position. I thought about the process – yes, I was now rewarded for the "end product," but what about the process? My thoughts led me back to the darkest times of my life. As I stretched my legs forward with the additional legroom of the first-class cabin, I realized that my grind and grit had finally paid off. It had morphed into a lifestyle that I never dreamed possible for myself. I sat next to a gentleman who was an executive salesperson, and he seemed fascinated by my reason for traveling. He was interested in me and my story. And, as we chatted, I couldn't help but flash that warehouse boyish smile and think, "Mom, look at me now."

I once had the opportunity to attend a Padres game in San Diego, California, and sit in the owner's private suite box. I never thought I would have the chance to experience such an outing. However, the game wasn't the main highlight; the fact that I was attending with my Commanding Officer was the true highlight. I remember getting there and seeing him arriving with his family. He had brought up his entire family and was very outwardly caring to each of them. He told me the importance of always including his family in his Navy journey. Throughout his career, he moved with his family each time and included them in all events and successes. I was very interested in hearing about his love of family because, until this point, I had always focused on work and the mission. I was sadly mistaken because having a work-life balance is the key to success. Later on, we were preparing to go to the owner's suite, but the Captain asked to take a detour for his young daughter. That day, she wanted a specific food.

The Captain was on a mission looking for some vendor in this huge ballpark with the specific food for his daughter. We went to at least three different floors and couldn't find one. Eventually, when we got to the next level, he tactfully negotiated with his daughter and got her to concede to an alternative but promised to make it up to her later. Who would've thought that a United States Commanding Officer of one of the greatest war-fighting machines would be flustered and nervous as he ran around for his daughter? Who would have thought that as a war-fighting leader, he had a heart bigger than the universe for his family? That day, I realized that he is not just a Commanding Officer but a father, husband, friend, and human with the same needs as everyone else. The bigger lesson here is despite how busy and demanding his duties were, he made time, and at no small cost, he put his daughter's happiness first.

Once we arrived at the owner's suite, I looked around, amazed at its fancy and exquisite food. The Captain asked if I wanted to eat, but I felt nervous and awkward in that environment, so I passed on the food. Noticing that I looked overwhelmed, the Captain said, "I know if I don't eat, you won't either, will you?" I glanced at him but remained silent. He continued, "Then we'll eat together." He made me feel comfortable, although I felt awkward in such a foreign environment. Soon after, an Admiral whom the Captain was familiar with entered the owner's suite and joined us. He began chatting with the Captain and asked, "How do you like your carrier tour?" The Captain responded that he loved the tour and realized that everything he learned during his Naval career was designed to prepare him for his tour as a U.S. Naval Aircraft-Carrier Commanding Officer. Listening to him and watching their interaction, I realized he had a mentor for 28 years of his highly accomplished Naval Career. He was a Commanding Officer with a mentor and is still a steward of learning. He never believed that he could not gain more knowledge; he felt someone could always teach him something else. We all, as leaders, should strive to learn, grow, and find a mentor. And remember what the Admiral said: "Everything you do in life is to prepare you for the next level."

FOOD FOR THOUGHT

Write about a person who has inspired you with their resilience. What qualities do they possess that you admire?

_____

_____

_____

_____

_____

_____

_____

_____

_____

_____

_____

_____

_____

_____

_____

_____

_____

_____

_____

_____

_____

_____

_____

_____

_____

_____

_____

I surround myself with positive influences that support my growth and well-being.

CHAPTER 5

NEVER GIVE UP

Some nights, I lay in bed, staring off into the distance and basking in the wonder of my journey. I think about all I have been through and endured and the struggle for significance that landed me here – in this life position. I think, "How could this poor, homeless orphan be this accomplished military leader with contagious energy and relentless passion? How could he be me?" It's almost as if I'm describing someone else to myself, but I see myself when I sit up and look at the reflection in my mirror.

Sometimes, as I look in that mirror, I'm reminded of the train in the classic children's tale, The Little Engine That Could. Instead of my reflection, I see a little train pushing and climbing uphill. I watch its struggle as it fights with all the obstacles along its path. I know that The Little Engine was "overworked and underpaid," but I see how much faith it had, and then I see myself – Mike Kwon. I am that Little Engine who reflects the American Dream of perseverance and optimism because, with all the challenges that blocked my path, I discovered ways to push and fight my way uphill to success.

When people think of the moral of this story, it's often forgotten that there is a less self-centered message embedded – when people need help, do your best to help them and don't give up. The Little Engine was trying to get over to the other side of the mountain to deliver toys to the children in time for Christmas. It knew that if the toys didn't make it, the children would be disappointed, and the Engine wouldn't allow that to happen, so it huffed and puffed its way over the mountain. We, as humans, should huff and puff to help others. The story is a gentle reminder about the difference we can make in the lives of others when we trust and believe in them. When I look in that same mirror, I see someone who is compassionate, empathetic, generous, diligent, and determined to be a change agent in the lives of others. And it's all because I learned a long time ago the importance of persistence – never giving up.

It begins with never forgetting where you came from because it provides the foundation of who you are and what you stand for. I will never forget sleeping in the subway station or on a cardboard box in an abandoned warehouse. It reminds me to appreciate my blessings now: a safe and secure home. Each day that I go to work, I know that I am working to ensure that I will never sleep on a cardboard box again, and this inspires me to continue working harder and smarter.

I've been uplifted watching the fruits of my labor as a drill instructor after the boot camp graduation ceremonies when I meet the families. Parents and loved ones often seek me out to thank me and share their appreciation for my leadership. With tears in their eyes, they share the transformation process of their Sailor and the impact that I had on the metamorphosis. It motivates me because they tell me about the difference I made in their lives, and it's a gentle reminder of my "why." Often, we only see it in small portions when we speak about leadership, training, coaching, etc. We lead in segments, and we coach in segments, but at graduation ceremonies, we can see the finished product among the graduates, and it's a phenomenal feeling. For me, it's a culmination of so many facets. Still, ultimately, it's about the finish — doing that proves you have never given up.

FOOD FOR THOUGHT

Describe a moment in your life when you felt most resilient. What factors contributed to your ability to bounce back from adversity?

_____

_____

_____

_____

_____

_____

_____

_____

_____

_____

_____

_____

_____

_____

_____

_____

_____

_____

_____

_____

_____

_____

_____

_____

_____

I am unstoppable, capable of achieving anything I set my mind to.

CHAPTER 6

FOR WHAT IT'S WORTH...

Have you ever been in an argument that starts with one topic, but by the end, you are discussing twenty other issues? Well, that happens when you lose focus of your "why" and forget why you are fighting and what your end goal is. To be a successful leader, you must always be focused and understand why you fight to make your own decisions. Is this easy? No. Is it necessary? Yes.

Remembering why we fight is essential and can motivate us to keep grinding until we reach our goals. What you are fighting for must be bigger than you: bigger than laziness, procrastination, obstacles, and adversities. It needs a Herculean strength that will empower you to view the word "No" as a starting point toward change and the tenacity to ask for the person who has the power to grant you a "Yes."

I learned this in my struggle for survival because I had no choice. I had to fight to eat, drink, sleep, and live daily, so my why was founded on the bare necessities in life. But you know what? It provided the foundation for me to excel in the military because I understood that I could never go back to being poor, homeless, feeling invisible, and like a "nobody." I knew that with every promotion I earned, I would receive more money, recognition, and respect. I didn't necessarily need the recognition, but it allowed me to move in circles where respect was guaranteed. This fueled my spirit – knowing that I wouldn't be passed over or ignored like a piece of dirt – I would never be homeless again.

If I had lost sight of the reason behind my fight as I navigated the world, I would not have achieved my level of success. I probably would have settled for a mediocre life because that's all I believed I deserved. Instead, I knew I wasn't designed to move backward to the left or right – my destination was only forward. I understand that when you hit rock bottom, there's no place to go but up. I had lived the rock bottom life already and fought to move up, so there was no way I planned to fall again. That's the "why" for my daily fight and keeps me going.

The great thing about remembering the why of my fight is that I get to teach and share with other military members. Sometimes, my Sailors need someone who understands their struggles for significance. They need someone who can help them figure out the reason for their fight for success. As their leader, I can be that guy and support them in reaching their pinnacles of success simply by working with them to understand the reason for their fight. It's the highlight of my current position – to motivate, inspire, encourage, and empower others to move toward positive change in their lives.

When recruits arrive at boot camp, they typically complete a "hard card entry" explaining why they chose to enter the military. The responses vary widely, but sometimes, I've used them to motivate myself to become a better leader. When frustrated, exhausted, or having a bad day, I read their entries for inspiration. I envision hope and excitement in their words, motivating me to grind. Their words often gently remind me of my "why" and passion. So, when we talk about leadership and our purpose, I know it's about helping others reach their next level.

FOOD FOR THOUGHT

Reflect on a time when you experienced a setback. How did you respond, and what did you learn from the experience?

_____
_____
_____
_____
_____
_____
_____
_____
_____
_____
_____
_____
_____
_____
_____
_____
_____
_____
_____
_____
_____
_____
_____
_____
_____

I focus on the present moment,
letting go of worries about the future.

CHAPTER 7

PURPOSE IN PERPETUITY

Purpose in perpetuity is the unwavering commitment to a lifelong journey of meaningful impact, where passion meets persistence, creating a legacy that transcends time and inspires a perpetual ripple of positive change. Some people live without a clear sense of purpose because they spend each day "surviving" and not "living." They fail to recognize and understand their true purpose in life, so they miss opportunities to be their best version. They may live their lives shrouded in fear, confusion, and doubt because they are not comfortable being uncomfortable. Never let that be you.

Seek out what gives you purpose, and then create life goals aligned with your purpose. My life story showed me that my purpose is to help others. From living in the warehouse canvassing for food daily to sharing with the other kids to mentoring young Sailors, I know God has put me here and used me to help others. As a result, everything I do is aligned with helping others.

I watched my mother, who had nothing, practically give everything she had to the church – her heart and soul and ask for nothing in return. She did it because it was the right thing to do, and she knew God blessed her with the gift to serve. Watching her, I knew I had inherited the gift, too. Servant Leadership is not just what I do; it's a part of who I am.

Walking in your purpose to infinity and beyond is necessary to be a good person and an effective leader. As I previously shared, your purpose must be clear if you want others to follow your path. Clarity only comes when you discover the heart of who you are, which allows you to fall in love with the process.

When we fall in love with the process, we find joy in the daily grind, appreciate the small victories, and have the resilience to push through challenges. It's about enjoying the journey, savoring each moment, and finding fulfillment in our progress. So, I encourage you to embrace the process, find passion in your work, and relish the journey towards your goals. When you do that, success becomes more than just an outcome; it becomes a way of life.

Your journey as a leader isn't a sprint; it's a marathon fueled by a passion that withstands the test of time. Embrace that your purpose is not a fixed destination but a constant evolution, a guiding force propelling you forward. It's about embracing challenges as opportunities, leading authentically, and channeling your unique blend of skills and passions into a force that leaves an indelible mark on the world. As you pursue your purpose, remember that genuine leadership is not just about the destination but the transformative journey you undertake—inspiring those around you and yourself, propelling the flame of purpose in perpetuity.

FOOD FOR THOUGHT

Imagine yourself living your ideal life ten years from now. What steps can you take today to move closer to that vision?

_____

_____

_____

_____

_____

_____

_____

_____

_____

_____

_____

_____

_____

_____

_____

_____

_____

_____

_____

_____

_____

_____

_____

_____

_____

I believe in my ability to create

a bright and fulfilling future.

CONCLUSION

My challenge for leaders is to learn how to inspire, give back, value people, and genuinely learn to connect with people. Leadership isn't just barking orders or demanding respect because you have authority. You must show that you care for their success and well-being.

When someone asks me where I learned these leadership and life skills, I tell them that life is like a steam catapult on an aircraft carrier. It takes precision work on the deck's machinery equipment; it takes an incredible job on the jet aircraft; it takes a strong and professional pilot to fly the aircraft, and wind, temperature, and different dynamics make all the difference in an ability to shoot a live aircraft in the middle of the ocean off a carrier. However, there is one key component that young folks work on called a steam catapult, and each shot requires a ton of steam to get a 50,000-plus pound aircraft airborne. Everyone needs that steam, that extra push, to get someone airborne. You should be that steam in someone's life. And be the steam to help someone go forward and go airborne. If not, people will sink and fall off the edge.

Looking back, various individuals played pivotal roles in my life, acting as the driving force behind my success. From social workers to foster care parents, high school counselors, and mentors, their support propelled me forward. These individuals, including leaders like Captain Crozier, provided the necessary push to soar. Though we come from diverse backgrounds, the willingness to serve and care for others is invaluable. It costs nothing to make a difference and provide that essential push for someone to thrive. Life's greatest treasure is being the energy for someone else, irrespective of our challenges. My life story, "From Homeless to Unstoppable," reflects on my journey from abandonment and surviving homelessness at 13 to becoming a successful military officer dedicated to giving back. Through this book, I've shared the highs, lows, struggles, triumphs, and valuable lessons learned along the way. I hope my words have served as a source of inspiration and motivation. Regardless of your circumstances, remember that you can rise above any challenge, persevere through hardship, and achieve your dreams.

As you complete this book, remember that it is significant to give back to others. Your generosity can profoundly impact them through small acts of kindness or more sizable contributions. And remember, throughout life's journey, trust the process. Obstacles, setbacks, and moments of doubt are all part of your growth and development, but keep moving forward with determination and resilience because each step brings you closer to your goals. No matter how imperfect they seem, embracing opportunities can lead to success. Sometimes, the first option may not be ideal, but what you make of it matters.

With hard work and grit, I excelled in the military, and now, as a speaker, I give back to thousands of people. Whenever I travel and speak, people often ask, "How did you survive?" and "What is Grit?" My answer is always the same: Grit is the ability to have passion and persevere over long periods. It's about working hard even when you can't see the result." This is one of the reasons why faith and hope are so challenging—they require belief in the unseen. In my life, I've tried to hold on to my faith with the hope of making a difference in the lives of others. Thank you for joining me on this journey. And, remember, life is what you make of it. Embrace each challenge, persevere passionately, and create the life you envision. Now, go out and make a difference!

NOTES

NOTES

NOTES

NOTES

NOTES

NOTES

NOTES

NOTES

NOTES

NOTES

ABOUT THE AUTHOR

Mike Kwon has two decades of professional experience in life coaching, speaking, and leadership development. With a proven track record of success, Mike has helped countless individuals and organizations reach their goals and achieve their full potential.

At 26, Mike embarked on his first professional speaking journey at a leadership conference, where he presented as part of a five-speaker lineup that included four CEOs. This early start in his speaking career shows his commitment to sharing his story and wisdom with others. It demonstrates his dedication to helping individuals and organizations develop their leadership skills and reach their full potential. Mike's authenticity is evident in his passion as an orator. His experiences and coaching are not just theoretical concepts but are rooted in real-life situations.

This authenticity shines through and resonates with his audience, making his talks impactful and memorable. His energy and enthusiasm are contagious, creating an atmosphere that motivates and inspires everyone in the crowd.

Mike received his Bachelor's degree in Organizational Leadership and a Master's in Business Leadership from the University of Charleston. Additionally, he accepted the prestigious Navy-wide Aviation Leadership Award, triumphing over 20,000 candidates.

59658114R00046